The Spark of Your Relationship

Adrian Collins

Copyright Page

First edition
All Rights Reserved
Author: © 2024, Adrian Collins

Index

Remembering the First Moments

Remembering the first moments of a relationship can be like opening an old photo album full of emotions. Those days were filled with spontaneous laughter, knowing glances, and an energy that seemed inexhaustible. The initial spark is that moment when everything seems magical and when two people find something special in each other. But over time, responsibilities, routines, and small everyday conflicts can overshadow that magic. This chapter is about how to reconnect with those moments and use them as a solid foundation to revitalize love.

The first step is to stop and think back. Do you remember how you met? What was it about your partner that attracted you? Maybe it was their infectious laugh, their way of talking, or a look that said more than a thousand words. Going back to those moments doesn't mean getting stuck in the past, but rather bringing back those emotions that brought you together in the first place. Often, couples forget why they fell in love. Life gets filled with distractions and the original reasons for your connection get buried under routine. Take time to reflect on those days. You can do it alone or together with your partner, sharing memories and reliving the details that made that time special.

Another way to remember those first moments is to talk about them openly. Tell your partner what you liked most about them when you first met. Ask them the same questions. Often, these conversations are a reminder of the foundation you built your relationship on. They can bring laughter, tears of joy, and a sense of gratitude for everything you've experienced together. By doing so, you're not only reminiscing, but also strengthening your current connection.

Recreating early experiences can also be a powerful way to get the spark back. If you used to go out to a certain place, like a café, a park, or a beach, consider visiting it again. Nostalgia can be a strong tool to rekindle emotions. It's not about copying exactly what you did before, but about reliving the essence of those moments. Even if circumstances have changed, the act of trying is already a gesture of love and commitment.

Also, reflect on what your attitude was like back in the day. Do you remember how hard you tried to make your partner laugh? Or how much effort you put into planning a special date? Over time, many couples stop doing these things because they become comfortable, and while comfort is positive in many ways, it can take away from the excitement. Get that winning attitude back, not because you need it, but because your partner deserves it. The initial spark doesn't go away, it just gets buried under the monotony, and small gestures can bring it out again.

It's important not to fall into the trap of comparing the past to the present. It's not about saying "it was better before," but about recognizing that what you experienced was beautiful and that same magic can be adapted to your current life. You've changed, you've grown, and you've faced challenges together. That doesn't take away from who you are now as a couple; in fact, it enriches it. Remembering the first moments shouldn't be an excuse to regret it, but rather an opportunity to celebrate how far you've come and use that energy to build something even better.

Finally, take this exercise of remembering as a step to look forward with excitement. Those first moments were the beginning of something great, and there is still room to write more chapters together. The spark of your relationship is not just a memory, it is an energy that can be rekindled again and again. Use memories as fuel for new adventures, new dreams, and new ways to tell your partner: "I choose you every day."

What Happened to Us?

What happened to us? This is a question that many couples ask themselves when they feel that the spark that united them has gone out or that their relationship no longer has the same energy as before. It is a question that can be difficult to face, because it brings with it a mix of emotions: sadness, frustration, confusion, and even fear. However, asking this question is an important step towards a solution. Recognizing that something has changed is the first step to working on recovering what was lost.

Burnout in a relationship doesn't happen overnight. It's a gradual process that can be so subtle that it goes unnoticed. It often starts with small things: conversations become less frequent or less deep, gestures of affection become scarce, shared laughter fades into routine, and quality moments are displaced by responsibilities, technology, or just plain tiredness. All of this can build up over time and create an emotional disconnect that feels hard to overcome.

One of the most common reasons for burnout is a lack of communication. At the beginning of a relationship, couples often talk about everything: dreams, fears, anecdotes, plans. But over time, conversations can be reduced to the practical: what to buy at the supermarket, who will pick up the kids, or what bill is due. Not only does this limit emotional connection, but it can also create a sense of distance. When we stop sharing our deepest thoughts and feelings, the relationship loses an important part of its essence.

Another common culprit is routine. Couples fall into habits that, while necessary to maintain an organized life, can become repetitive and boring. Going out to work, coming home, eating dinner in front of the TV, and repeating the cycle day after day can rob a relationship of its sense of adventure and excitement. Routine isn't the enemy, but when it completely dominates a couple's dynamic, it can stifle romance.

There are also unresolved conflicts. Sometimes couples avoid talking about sensitive topics to avoid arguments, but this only creates a buildup of tension that sooner or later explodes. Those small resentments that are pushed aside because "it's not worth arguing about" can become emotional barriers over time. Even if they are not talked about, they are there, affecting the way you interact.

Finally, there's the issue of neglect. Not necessarily physical neglect, although that can also play a role, but emotional neglect. Over time, some couples stop making the effort to show affection or interest. Things like saying "I love you," giving an unexpected hug, or planning a special date may seem less important when the relationship has been going on for years. But the reality is that these small gestures are the glue that holds a couple together.

So, what happened to us? Life happened. Responsibilities, stress, routines, and distractions happened. Days passed when we didn't have the time or energy to prioritize ourselves as a couple. But the important thing is not just to understand what happened, but to decide what to do about it. This moment of reflection should not be a sentence, but a starting point to work together to reconnect.

Talking honestly about what you feel and what you think has changed is crucial. It may be uncomfortable at first, but it's the only way to understand each other better. It's also important to look beyond complaints and think of solutions. Maybe you need more quality time together, maybe you need to rediscover what makes you happy as a couple, or maybe you need to forgive each other for past mistakes. What matters is taking action.

The good news is that if you are willing to work at it, getting back what you have lost is possible. Love doesn't go away; it just gets buried beneath the layers of everyday life. This chapter is an invitation to peel back those layers and find again what made you say "yes" to each other. What happened to us? What happened is not the end, it is an opportunity to start over.

Effective Communication

Effective communication is at the heart of any healthy relationship. It's like the bridge that connects two worlds, allowing emotions, thoughts, and desires to flow freely. However, when that bridge is broken or weakened, connections are lost and misunderstandings grow like weeds. In this chapter, we're going to explore what it means to communicate effectively and how it can transform a relationship that feels disconnected.

First, we need to understand what communication really is. It's not just about talking, but about getting a message across in a way that's understood and receiving the other person's message with attention. This is where many couples stumble. They may think they're talking a lot, but if they're not listening or if what they're saying isn't clear, that communication isn't working. For example, when one partner says, "You never help me," and the other responds, "I'm always busy," they're just accusing each other instead of solving the problem.

A big mistake in communication is assuming that the other person knows what we're thinking or feeling. None of us has a crystal ball. Saying "you should know" is unfair. If something is bothering you or you need something from your partner, say it clearly. For example, instead of saying "you never pay attention to me," you could say "I wish you'd pay attention to me when I talk to you, it makes me feel important." Not only does this communicate the problem, it also points to a solution.

The way we speak matters, too. Words can build or destroy. Speaking respectfully, even in the middle of an argument, is essential. Swearing, yelling, or speaking sarcastically won't make your partner listen to you better; on the contrary, it will put him or her on the defensive. If you're upset, take a deep breath before you speak. Use phrases that begin with "I feel" instead of "you always." Saying "I feel ignored when you're on the phone at dinner" is much more effective than yelling "you're always glued to the phone!"

But talking is only part of the equation. Listening is just as important, and it's not just about hearing the words, but understanding the message behind them.

Active listening means paying attention, not interrupting, and trying to understand what your partner is saying, even if you don't agree. Often, while the other person is talking, we're already thinking about what we're going to say in response. This isn't listening; it's debating. Take a moment to process what you hear before you respond.

Also, consider nonverbal language. Words are important, but gestures, facial expressions, and tone of voice also communicate a lot. You can say, "I'm not upset," but if your tone is cold and you're crossing your arms, your partner will receive a completely different message. Learn to be consistent with what you say and how you say it. And, likewise, pay attention to your partner's nonverbal language. Sometimes, what is not said is just as important as what is said.

Another key aspect of effective communication is choosing the right time and place to talk. Don't try to have a serious conversation when you're both tired, rushed, or distracted. If there's something important to discuss, find a time when you can both be calm and focused. Also, avoid arguing in public or in front of other people—this only adds tension and can make both of you feel exposed.

It's also important to learn how to say sorry and accept apologies. No one is perfect, and making mistakes is part of any relationship. Saying "I'm sorry" when you mess up not only shows maturity, but it also opens the door for your partner to feel safe expressing their feelings. On the other hand, accepting an apology doesn't mean holding a grudge. If you forgive, do so sincerely and move on from the issue.

Finally, don't forget the power of small gestures of positive communication. A text message during the day, a sincere "thank you," or an "I love how you do this" can reinforce the emotional connection. Not everything has to be a deep conversation; sometimes a simple gesture shows your partner that you're thinking about them and care.

Effective communication isn't something that happens automatically, especially after years of relationship. It takes effort, patience, and practice. But the reward is invaluable: a relationship where both of you feel heard, valued, and connected. So start today. Talk, listen, understand, and rebuild that bridge that unites your worlds. Your relationship is worth it.

Understanding to Love Better

Understanding in order to love better is a principle that can transform any relationship. Often, in love, we take for granted that we know our partner. We think we understand what they want, what they feel, and what they need. But the reality is that people change, evolve, and have nuances that we sometimes overlook. Loving better doesn't just mean giving more love; it means understanding the person at your side more deeply, and that understanding requires time, patience, and attention.

For starters, understanding isn't the same as assuming. Sometimes we think we know why our partner is acting a certain way or what they're thinking, but those assumptions are often based on our own perceptions and not what's really going on inside. For example, if your partner is quiet, you might assume they're upset with you, but maybe they're dealing with a problem at work or just need some quiet time. To avoid misunderstandings, it's important to ask rather than guess. A simple question like, "Are you okay? Is there anything you'd like to share?" can open the door to an honest conversation.

Understanding also involves listening with intent. Not just hearing the words, but picking up on the message behind them. Sometimes people don't directly express what they feel because they don't know how or they're afraid of being judged. For example, when your partner says, "You're always busy," they might actually be saying, "I feel ignored." If you listen with an open heart, you can respond in a way that not only solves the immediate problem, but also strengthens the relationship.

Additionally, it's important to remember that we all have different ways of expressing and receiving love. Gary Chapman, in his theory of the five love languages, explains that some people feel loved through words of affirmation, while others value acts of service, quality time, gifts, or physical touch more. If you don't understand your partner's love language, you may both end up frustrated. For example, you might be buying your partner expensive gifts thinking that it shows your love, when what they really need is for you to spend more time with them. Knowing your partner's love language is a powerful way to show that you care.

Another key to better understanding your partner is knowing their history. We all carry experiences, beliefs, and hurts from our past that shape who we are and how we relate to each other. Maybe your partner avoids conflict because they grew up in a home where arguments were constant and painful. Maybe they have a hard time expressing their emotions because they never learned to do so. Understanding where they're coming from will allow you to see beyond their actions and understand the reasons behind them. This doesn't mean justifying negative behaviors, but it will help you approach them with empathy instead of anger.

Empathy is key to understanding and loving better. Putting yourself in your partner's shoes means imagining how they feel from their perspective, not yours. If they had a bad day at work, instead of minimizing it by saying, "It's no big deal," try validating their emotions with something like, "That must have been really hard for you." These types of responses not only show that you care, but they also strengthen trust and emotional connection.

It's also essential to accept that you don't always have to agree with your partner to understand them. In any relationship, there will be differences of opinion, values, or priorities. The key is not to change the other person, but to accept their views and find common ground. For example, if one of you prefers to spend weekends at home and the other wants to go out, you can find a balance by alternating activities that you both enjoy. Mutual respect is the basis for dealing with these differences without them turning into conflict.

Finally, understanding your partner requires ongoing effort. It's not enough to know each other well at the beginning of the relationship and assume that information will be valid forever. People grow, change, and face new challenges, which means there's always something new to learn. Regularly ask them how they feel, what's bothering them, what makes them happy. These small efforts to understand can make a big difference in how they feel loved and valued.

Understanding how to love better isn't just advice; it's a commitment you can make to your partner and to yourself. By taking the time and attention to truly understand who the person next to you is, you'll not only strengthen your relationship, but you'll also discover a deeper level of love and connection that you may not have known existed. This understanding is not only the foundation for a happier relationship, but also for a more meaningful life together.

Small Gestures, Big Impacts

Sometimes we think that to strengthen a relationship or to rekindle the spark of love we need grand gestures, such as exotic trips, expensive dinners or impressive gifts. However, it is the small, everyday gestures that can really make a difference. These simple, but intentional details are like drops of water that nourish love and connection day after day. In this chapter we are going to explore how small gestures can have big impacts on your relationship.

Let's start with something as basic as a "thank you." As our routine progresses, we stop thanking for the little things. We forget to say, "thank you for making breakfast," "thank you for taking the kids to school," or "thank you for listening to me when I was having a bad day." These words are powerful because they acknowledge the other person's effort and make them feel that what they do matters. Don't underestimate the power of a "thank you"; it can be the detail that transforms an ordinary day into a special one.

Another simple but meaningful gesture is an unexpected hug. Physical contact is a form of communication that doesn't require words. A hug can convey affection, support, comfort, or simply say "I'm here for you." Sometimes, after a difficult day, a sincere hug is worth more than any speech. Don't wait for your partner to ask for it; offer it spontaneously. A hug in the morning, when you get home, or before bed can greatly strengthen the emotional bond.

Text messages are also a powerful tool. A simple "I was thinking about you" or "I hope you have a great day" can brighten your partner's day. You don't need to write something elaborate; the important thing is that you show that you care. These little reminders that you're there, even when you're not together, can help keep the connection alive.

Acts of service are another way to show love in simple ways. It can be something as small as making a cup of coffee, picking up something you know your partner needs, or taking care of a task that your partner normally does. It doesn't have to be a huge effort; the important thing is that your partner sees that you thought about them and wanted to lighten their load, even if just a little.

Paying attention to details is also a gesture that can have a big impact. If you know your partner likes a certain type of chocolate, buy it for them when you go to the grocery store. If they like a particular song, play it in the background while you're having dinner. If they mentioned that they want to read a specific book, surprise them by buying it for them. These small acts show that you pay attention to their tastes and desires, which strengthens the bond between you both.

Quality time, even if it's brief, is also an important gesture. You don't need to spend hours; sometimes a few minutes of mindfulness can be enough. Turn off your phone, put aside distractions, and listen to your partner. Ask how their day was and really listen to the answer. This type of connection, even if it seems simple, reinforces the message that your partner is important to you.

Let's not forget the power of kind words. A genuine compliment, such as "you look amazing today" or "I love the way you do that," can boost your partner's mood and remind them that you appreciate them. Over time, many couples stop complimenting each other, but getting back into the habit can have a huge impact on how you feel about each other.

Sometimes, small gestures can also include giving your partner space. If you notice that your partner is overwhelmed, offering to babysit so they have some quiet time or suggesting that they take some time for themselves can be a huge act of love. Showing empathy and understanding when someone needs a break is also a way to nurture your bond.

Finally, don't underestimate the power of a smile. Smiling at your partner, even in the middle of a busy day, is a silent reminder that you're happy to share your life with them. It's a gesture that costs nothing, but can convey a lot. A smile can ease tensions, convey affection, and remind your partner that, despite everything, the love is still there.

In short, you don't need to go to great lengths to have a big impact on your relationship. Small gestures, when done with intention and love, can be more powerful than you might imagine. These everyday details are like bricks that build a strong, lasting relationship. So start today, with something as simple as a hug, a thank you, or a smile. Your partner will notice, and the impact will be bigger than you expect.

Healing Past Wounds

Healing past wounds is one of the most important and, at the same time, most difficult steps in a relationship. When we have been hurt or when we have hurt, emotions such as resentment, pain and guilt can get trapped between us, creating a barrier that prevents love from flowing freely. No matter how much time has passed, if those wounds are not addressed, they will continue to affect the relationship in subtle but profound ways. This chapter is an invitation to face those wounds with courage, patience and commitment, because only by healing them can we move towards a fuller and more genuine love.

The first step to healing is to acknowledge that the wounds exist. Many times, we prefer to ignore them, thinking that time will make them disappear. But time does not heal what is not faced. If there is an issue from the past that still hurts you, even if you do not mention it, that pain can manifest itself in the form of mistrust, anger or indifference towards your partner. Do an exercise of introspection and ask yourself what situations or words left that emotional mark on you. Be honest with yourself, because only then can you begin to work on it.

After acknowledging your own wounds, it's important to open a space for communication with your partner. Talking about painful topics isn't easy, but it's necessary. Find a quiet moment, without distractions, and express what you feel calmly and clearly. Instead of blaming or attacking, focus on explaining how certain events affected you. For example, instead of saying, "You never supported me when I needed it," you could say, "I felt alone at that time and that hurt me a lot." This approach not only prevents a defensive reaction, but also makes it easier for your partner to understand how you feel.

Listening is just as important as talking. If your partner has past hurts, give them the space to share them with you. Avoid interrupting or minimizing what they say, even if you feel you didn't mean to hurt them. Remember that each person's perception of pain is unique, and validating what they're feeling is a crucial step in the healing process. Ask sincerely how you can help heal those hurts, and show that you're willing to make changes if necessary.

Forgiveness is a fundamental pillar of healing. This doesn't mean justifying what happened, but rather releasing the emotional weight you carry with you. If someone hurt you, resentment can become a burden that affects not only your relationship, but also yourself. Forgiveness isn't something that happens overnight, but you can take small steps. Reflect on what happened, acknowledge your own feelings, and, over time, decide to let go of that pain. Remember that forgiveness is not a gift for the other person, but for yourself, because it frees you from the past and allows you to live in the present.

If you were the one who hurt your partner, forgiveness also involves asking for it sincerely. A superficial "I'm sorry" isn't enough; your partner needs to feel that you understand the impact of your actions and that you are willing to work to not repeat them. Ask how you can repair the damage and demonstrate with concrete actions that you are committed to change. Forgiveness is not earned with words, but with perseverance and effort.

An important aspect of the healing process is learning from your hurts. Every experience, even the painful ones, has something to teach us. Reflect on what happened and look for lessons you can apply to strengthen your relationship. Maybe you learned the importance of communicating better, setting boundaries, or being more empathetic. Use these lessons to build a stronger, healthier relationship.

Patience is essential in this process. Healing doesn't happen immediately, and each person has his or her own pace. There will be days when you feel like you're moving forward, and other days when the wounds feel fresher than ever. This is normal. The important thing is to stay committed to the process, even when it's difficult. Remind yourself and your partner that you're both working toward a common goal: building a stronger, more authentic love.

Finally, remember that healing past wounds doesn't mean forgetting what happened, but rather transforming that pain into an opportunity to grow. Scars are a testament to what you've overcome together and can become a source of strength if you decide to face them as a team. By doing so, you'll not only be leaving the weight of the past behind, but also making room for a future full of love, trust, and hope.

Healing is an act of love, both towards yourself and towards your partner. Don't be afraid to face those wounds. On the contrary, consider it a brave and necessary step to recover the spark and build a stronger, more honest and deeper relationship.

Recognizing the Languages of Love

Recognizing love languages is one of the most important steps to strengthening a relationship and getting the spark back. Often, couples feel disconnected not because they don't love each other, but because they don't know how to express that love in a way that the other truly understands. It's like they speak different languages: one says "I love you" with words, but the other needs to see it in actions, and that's where things get complicated. This chapter will help you identify your love language, your partner's love language, and how to use them to connect more deeply.

The idea of love languages was developed by author Gary Chapman and posits that each person has a preferred way of receiving and giving love. These languages are words of affirmation, quality time, gifts, acts of service, and physical touch. Understanding what your partner's primary language is can be a real game-changer in your relationship, because it allows you to show love in the way they truly need it.

The first love language is words of affirmation. Some people need to hear that they are loved, valued, and appreciated. This doesn't mean giving empty compliments; it's about expressing sincere feelings. Phrases like "you make me so happy," "I love the way you solve problems," or "I admire you for your patience" can mean a lot to someone whose primary love language is words of affirmation. If your partner lights up when you say something nice to them or if they tend to use words to express their love, this may be their language.

The second language is quality time. For those who have this language, the most important thing is not just being together physically, but actually connecting. It's not about looking at your phone while you're in the same room, but about spending time together full of time without distractions. This can be having a meaningful conversation, going for a walk together, or just enjoying a leisurely meal. If your partner always asks you to spend more time with them or gets frustrated when you're present but distracted, this is probably their love language.

The third love language is gifts. Here it's not about the material value, but rather the meaning behind the gesture. A gift can be a tangible reminder that you thought of your partner. It can be something as simple as their favorite chocolate, a flower picked from the path, or an object that you know will make them smile. If your partner always saves things you give them or gets excited when you surprise them with something, even small, this may be their language.

The fourth language is acts of service. For some people, actions speak louder than words. Things like doing the dishes, helping with chores, babysitting so your partner can rest, or making their favorite meal can all be ways of saying "I love you." If your partner really appreciates it when you do practical things to make their life easier, this is probably their love language.

Finally, physical touch is the fifth language. This isn't limited to sexual intimacy; it includes things like hugging, cuddling, holding hands, or just sitting close to each other. For those who have this language, physical touch is a powerful way to connect emotionally. If your partner seeks out spontaneous hugs, holds your hand while walking, or leans in close to you when you're together, this is probably their language.

Once you identify your partner's primary language, the next step is to actively use it. You may realize that you've been showing love in ways that don't have as much impact on your partner. For example, you might be showering them with compliments (words of affirmation), but if their primary language is quality time, what they really need is for you to turn off your phone and talk to them. Making this shift can transform the dynamic of your relationship.

It's also important to recognize your own love language. We often give love in the language we prefer to receive it, but this doesn't always match what our partner needs. Talking about this openly can be revealing and help you understand yourself and your partner better. Ask yourself what actions or gestures make you feel most loved, and share this with your partner so they can demonstrate their love in ways that are meaningful to you.

Remember that people don't have just one love language. While one is often dominant, we all have a combination of all five. That's why diversifying your ways of showing love can also be beneficial. A hug in the morning, a kind word at midday, an act of service in the afternoon, and quality time in the evening can cover several bases and keep the spark alive.

Recognizing and speaking love languages isn't something that happens right away. It takes observation, communication, and practice, but the results are worth it. Once you both start expressing your love in the languages you truly understand, you're likely to feel a deeper connection and greater harmony in your relationship. This small effort can have a big impact, because love isn't just about feeling it, but about showing it in ways that the other can truly appreciate.

Quality Time

Quality time is one of the most valuable elements in any relationship. It's about so much more than just being together; it's about devoting your full attention to your partner and sharing meaningful moments that strengthen your connection. In today's fast-paced world, where work, social media, and daily responsibilities compete for our attention, quality time can become one of the hardest things to achieve, but also one of the most important. This chapter will help you understand what this concept really means and how you can incorporate it into your relationship to bring back the spark.

Spending quality time means being fully present with your partner. This means putting aside distractions and focusing solely on them. It's not about sitting in the same room while each of you looks at your phone or TV, but about sharing moments where you both are emotionally connected. It can be a deep conversation, an activity you enjoy together, or even something as simple as having a coffee while looking into each other's eyes. The key is how much attention you give your partner during that time.

For some people, quality time is their primary love language. This means that they value those moments where they feel like they have your undivided attention the most. If your partner tends to complain that they "never spend time together" or seems happiest when they do something together, this is likely their love language. In that case, spending quality time with each other isn't just a nice gesture, but an emotional necessity for them.

One of the best ways to create quality time is to plan activities that you both enjoy. This doesn't have to be expensive or complicated. It can be as simple as going for a walk, cooking together, playing a board game, or even working on a team project. The important thing is that you both actively participate and feel connected. If you're not sure what activity to choose, ask your partner what they'd like to do. Not only will this give you ideas, but it will also show them that you care about what they think.

Communication is an essential part of quality time. Take advantage of these moments to talk about your days, share thoughts and feelings, and listen to your partner without interruptions. Many times, people just need to be heard in order to feel valued. Ask questions, show genuine interest, and avoid giving advice unless asked. The idea isn't to solve problems, but to be present and show that you care about what your partner has to say.

Another effective way to spend quality time is to create daily or weekly rituals. It can be something as simple as taking five minutes every night to talk before bed, having breakfast together on the weekends, or going for a walk after work. These small rituals not only strengthen the connection, but they also create a regular space where you both can focus on each other.

Quality time doesn't always have to be long. Even a few minutes a day can make a big difference if you use them well. For example, instead of being distracted while your partner is telling you something, stop what you're doing and look into their eyes. That simple gesture can make them feel valued and loved. Quality will always be more important than quantity.

On the other hand, it's important to mention that not all activities count as quality time. If you're physically present but mentally absent, your partner will notice. This includes things like checking your phone, being preoccupied with work, or simply not showing interest. For quality time to be effective, you need to be fully present, both physically and emotionally.

It's also essential to recognize that quality time doesn't always have to be perfect. There will be days when you're tired, when conversations aren't flowing, or when you just don't feel like doing much. That's okay. The important thing is that you continue to prioritize those moments together and that you both know that you're making an effort to connect.

Lastly, remember that quality time is a gift you give to yourself and your relationship. Not only does it strengthen your bond with your partner, but it also allows you to disconnect from daily worries and enjoy what really matters. By dedicating these meaningful moments, you are investing in the health and happiness of your relationship, which is one of the most valuable things you can do.

Quality time doesn't require grand gestures or elaborate planning. All you need is your attention, your willingness, and your love. At the end of the day, what really matters is not how much time you spent together, but how you spent it. Every quality moment is an opportunity to reconnect, to remember why you chose each other, and to continue building a relationship full of love and meaning.

Breaking the Routine

Routine is one of the deadliest things to a relationship. At first, everything feels exciting and new, but over time, daily life can become monotonous. Without realizing it, we fall into a cycle of repetitive habits that, while practical, can cause the spark to die out. Breaking routine is not only important to keep a relationship alive, but also to remind each other why you fell in love in the first place. This chapter will show you how to identify when routine is affecting your relationship and how you can put a fresh and exciting spin on it.

First, you have to understand how routine manifests itself. It's not just doing the same thing every day; it's stopping doing special things. It's when conversations are limited to the basics, like what to buy at the grocery store or who will pick up the kids. It's when couples' nights turn into sitting in front of the TV without really interacting. Routine is also noticeable in the little details we stop taking care of, like surprising your partner or taking a moment to express how much you love them.

Breaking the routine doesn't mean changing everything you do, nor does it mean doing something extreme. It's about making small changes that add novelty and excitement to your daily routine. For example, if you always eat dinner at home, go out to eat somewhere you've never tried before. If you always watch TV after dinner, replace that time with a walk together or a board game. These small adjustments may seem insignificant, but they have a huge impact because they break the predictable pattern.

One of the most effective ways to break up the routine is to try something completely new together. This could be an activity, such as taking a dance class, going rock climbing, cooking a different recipe, or even taking a spontaneous trip. The idea is to get out of your comfort zone and share an experience that gives you something new to talk about and remember. Doing something new is not only fun, but it also strengthens your bond because you're both facing something new together.

If leaving the house isn't possible, you can break the routine from the comfort of home. Plan a surprise date for your partner. For example, prepare a romantic dinner, play music you both like, and turn off your phones. If you have children, wait until they're asleep so you can have some alone time. You can also relive happy memories, like looking at photos of special moments or recreating your first date. These small actions help you remember why you're together and rekindle your connection.

Another way to break out of the monotony is to change the way you interact. If you're normally serious, try being more playful. Make jokes, send each other unexpected messages during the day, or plan something just to surprise each other. If you have a habit of being silent in the mornings, try starting the day with light conversation or some feel-good music. Changes in how you communicate can also bring freshness to your relationship.

One important thing to remember is not to underestimate the power of small details. Small surprises, like leaving a loving note, bringing their favorite dessert, or simply saying something nice, can make a big difference. Often, couples think they need big gestures to change things, but many times it's these small actions that have the biggest impact because they show that you're thinking about your partner and that you care about keeping the connection alive.

It's normal for routine to set in in a relationship, but you don't want to let it take over. The key is to be proactive. Talk openly about how you're feeling and what you can do to change things up. Often, just planning something together creates excitement. For example, talk about places you'd like to visit, things you've always wanted to try, or activities you used to enjoy but have stopped doing.

Breaking the routine is also about attitude. Instead of seeing daily tasks as tedious, try to find ways to make them more enjoyable. For example, if you have to clean the house, put on some music and do it together. If one of you has to cook, the other can join you and make it a time to talk. It's not always about changing what you do, but how you do it.

It's important to remember that breaking routine isn't a one-time effort; it's something you need to do continually. Over time, even new activities can become routine if you don't give them variety. That's why it's essential to always be aware of how you're feeling and look for ways to keep the relationship interesting. It's not about doing something spectacular every day, but about finding small ways to surprise each other and stay connected.

Ultimately, breaking the routine not only revitalizes your relationship, but it also allows you to rediscover yourselves as a couple. It's a way to remember that while life may be predictable, your relationship doesn't have to be. When you make the effort to break out of the monotony, you're investing in your happiness as a couple and creating memories that will help keep the spark of love alive.

Renewing Intimacy

Intimacy is one of the fundamental pillars of any relationship, but it is also one of the aspects that can be most easily affected over time. Daily responsibilities, stress, routine, and lack of communication can cool what was once a connection full of passion and closeness. Renewing intimacy is not only about the physical aspect, but also about recovering that emotional connection that made you feel special and unique to each other. This chapter is an invitation to explore simple and effective ways to strengthen that intimacy and rediscover the pleasure of being together.

First, it's important to understand that intimacy isn't limited to physical touch. It includes the way you look at each other, talk to each other, and care for each other. It starts with trust and vulnerability. If you feel like there's an emotional barrier between you, take the time to open up and talk about what you're feeling. Sometimes, simply expressing what's bothering you or what you need can be the first step to getting closer again. Talk about what makes you feel loved, what hurts you, and what you want back in your relationship.

Making time for yourself and your partner is essential. In the day-to-day, it's easy to let everything else take priority, but your relationship needs constant attention. Plan times when you can be alone, without distractions. It can be something as simple as sitting down for coffee in the kitchen or a special date out of the house. The important thing is that you're both present in the moment, listening to each other and enjoying each other's company.

Physical touch is a powerful language in intimacy. Sometimes, over time, we stop giving spontaneous hugs, holding hands, or kissing with the same passion. Getting back to these small actions can make a big difference. A long, sincere hug, an unexpected kiss, or simply stroking your partner's hand while talking are gestures that reaffirm affection and connection. Don't underestimate the power of these small displays of affection; they are like the glue that holds the relationship together.

Renewing intimacy also means being creative and breaking up the monotony. If your sex life has become predictable or non-existent, it's time to change things up. Talk openly about your desires, what you'd like to try, or what you feel is missing. Communication is key here, as intimacy issues often arise because we don't express what we need or we fear being judged. Explore new ways to connect physically, but always make sure you both feel comfortable and respected.

Another powerful way to renew intimacy is to rekindle the romance. Romantic details don't have to be grand or expensive, but they do have to be meaningful. Surprise your partner with a love note, a special dinner, or a loving message during the day. Sometimes the simplest gestures are the most impactful because they show that you thought of them. Reminding your partner how much you value them and how much they mean to you is essential to strengthening the connection.

Intimacy also thrives on shared fun. Laughing together creates a unique bond. Think of activities you both enjoy, whether it's watching a funny movie, playing a game together, or just reminiscing about funny times from the past. Laughter not only relieves tension, but it also reminds you that being together is something worth enjoying. Fun and joy are elements that, although sometimes forgotten, are essential to a healthy relationship.

One aspect that is often overlooked is the importance of taking care of yourself to improve your relationship. When you feel good about yourself, it is easier to give yourself completely to your partner. This includes both physical and emotional care. Make time to do things that make you happy, relax you, and energize you. A person who feels fulfilled with themselves has more to offer others.

Finally, renewing intimacy requires patience and commitment. Don't expect things to change overnight. There will be good days and bad days, but the important thing is to not give up. Every small step you take to get closer will make the relationship stronger. Remember that intimacy is an ongoing process and that mutual effort is what keeps that special spark alive.

Renewing intimacy is not about going back to what you were at the beginning, but about discovering a new stage in your relationship together. It is an opportunity to grow as a couple, to get to know each other in new ways, and to reaffirm the love that brought you together. No matter how long you have been together, there is always room to rediscover each other and rekindle that special connection that makes you unique.

The Balance Between the Self and the We

In a relationship, finding the balance between me and we can be a constant challenge. Loving someone and sharing life together doesn't mean losing yourself in the process. On the contrary, a healthy relationship requires each person to maintain their individuality while building a strong bond with the other. This balance is crucial to maintaining the spark of love and ensuring that the relationship doesn't become a burden, but a space where both can grow and flourish.

It's important to start by recognizing that each person is a unique being with their own dreams, goals, interests, and needs. While the relationship is a priority, it's also essential to make time for yourself. This doesn't mean being selfish or disinterested, but rather understanding that in order to give your best to your partner, you must first be at peace with yourself. If you neglect your own needs, over time, you may begin to feel resentment or dissatisfaction, which inevitably affects the relationship.

To maintain this balance, make time for your hobbies, projects, and friendships. If you're passionate about reading, sports, art, or any other activity, don't neglect those things that make you happy. These activities not only recharge you, but they also help you maintain your own identity within the relationship. Talking to your partner about what you enjoy doing alone is also important so that you both understand the need for these personal spaces.

On the other hand, the "we" in a relationship involves sharing, building together, and supporting each other. This includes making decisions together, having common goals, and spending quality time. The balance is found in knowing when to prioritize time as a couple and when to prioritize your individual needs. It's not about competing for space or attention, but rather collaborating so that both feel fulfilled.

Open communication is key to maintaining this balance. Talk about what you both need as individuals and as a couple. Sometimes, one of you may feel neglected because the other is too focused on their own interests, or you may feel like you don't have enough personal space. Being honest about these emotions and working together to find a middle ground is essential. Listening without judgment and being empathetic toward each other's needs can make a big difference.

Balance is also reflected in how you handle shared responsibilities. In many relationships, one partner may end up shouldering more of the burden than the other, which can lead to frustration. Divide up tasks fairly, taking into account both partners' abilities and schedules. When responsibilities are evenly distributed, it's easier for both partners to have time and energy to devote to their individual interests as well as to the relationship.

Also, the balance between me and we involves respecting differences. In a relationship, you won't always agree on everything, and that's okay. The important thing is to learn to accept those differences without trying to change them. This also includes giving each other space to have moments of solitude or to share with other people. Feeling jealous or insecure about these moments can be a sign that the balance isn't working well, and it's something you need to address together.

Remember that a relationship should not be the only source of happiness in your life. It is natural to want your partner to make you happy, but it is also important to be able to find that happiness within yourself. When both of you are responsible for your own happiness and share it with each other, the relationship becomes stronger and healthier. Don't put all the pressure of your emotional well-being on the relationship, because that can create unnecessary tension.

Finally, the balance between me and we takes patience and practice. It won't always be perfect, and there will be times when one of you needs more attention or more space. The important thing is to be willing to adapt and find solutions that work for both of you. Remember that love isn't about losing yourself in each other, but about walking together, supporting and respecting each other as individuals.

Maintaining this balance not only benefits the relationship, but also each person as a person. A couple where both have room to grow, both together and separately, has a better chance of maintaining the spark of love over time. Because in the end, a healthy relationship is one in which two complete people choose to share their lives, not because they need to, but because they want to.

The Importance of Humor in Love

Humor is one of the most powerful tools to keep the spark alive in a relationship. It's not just about making your partner laugh or telling jokes all the time, but about learning to find moments of joy even in the midst of difficulties. A relationship that lacks humor can become too serious or tense, which can lead to small differences turning into big conflicts. Instead, when humor is present, life as a couple feels lighter, more enjoyable, and more connected.

Laughing together is a way to create happy memories. Think of those times when an unexpected joke or a silly mistake made you laugh out loud. These moments not only relieve stress, but they also strengthen the bond between you. When you laugh with someone, you are sharing a genuine moment of connection. Humor has the ability to disarm tensions and remind us that not everything in life has to be so serious.

In a relationship, problems are inevitable. There will be days when things don't go as expected, when plans are ruined, or when the little frustrations of everyday life catch up with you. That's where humor can make all the difference. Instead of letting a misunderstanding turn into a fight or a mistake become a cause for resentment, learning to laugh at the situation can completely change the mood. For example, if you get lost on the way somewhere, instead of getting frustrated, you can joke about your "unexpected adventure." These little gestures of humor can prevent problems from escalating unnecessarily.

Furthermore, humor has a positive effect on how we perceive our partner. Seeing someone laugh, especially when it's an authentic, genuine laugh, reminds us of why we fell in love with that person. Laughter has a transformative power, as it makes us see our partner in a warmer, more human light. In those moments, we stop focusing on small imperfections and remember the joy of sharing our lives with someone who makes us feel good.

Humor can also be a tool for dealing with sensitive topics. There are times when certain conversations can feel awkward or tense. Introducing a little humor, in a respectful and loving way, can ease the tension and make both of you feel more comfortable. For example, if your partner forgot something important, instead of making a drama out of it, you can joke around by saying something like, "Well, I think we officially named you the king of forgetfulness today." Not only does this get the message across, but it does so in a less confrontational way.

However, it's important to understand that humor in a relationship should always be respectful. Making jokes about your partner's feelings or insecurities is not humor, it's insensitivity. Humor should unite, not divide. Before making a joke, consider how your partner might feel. If there's any doubt about whether it might hurt their feelings, it's best to avoid it. Humor that strengthens the relationship is one that both of you enjoy and that leaves no room for resentment.

In addition to being a tool for coping with challenges, humor is also a way to celebrate life together. Laughter doesn't have to be reserved only for difficult times. Doing silly things together, like dancing around the living room or making up silly songs while cooking, can be a wonderful way to enjoy each other's company. These little moments of joy are like glue that holds a couple together.

Humor also teaches us not to take ourselves too seriously. In a relationship, there will be times when you do something embarrassing or wrong. Instead of feeling bad about it, learn to laugh at yourself. Not only does this help you take the pressure off, but it also shows your partner that you are someone who is easy to live with. When you both can laugh at your own mistakes, it creates an environment of acceptance and comfort.

Finally, humor doesn't have to be something that happens spontaneously. If you feel like you've lost some of the joy in your relationship, you can find activities that make you laugh together. Watching a funny movie, playing a fun game, or reminiscing about funny moments from the past can all be ways to reintroduce humor into your relationship. The key is to be willing to look for those moments and allow the laughter to flow.

Humor is like a spark that ignites joy in love. It doesn't require effort or excessive planning, just a willingness to see the funny side of life and share it with your partner. Laughing together not only lightens problems, but also strengthens love. Because in the end, love is not just a place to feel safe, it is also a space to have fun and enjoy.

Shared Dreams

Shared dreams are the engine of a strong and lasting relationship. Dreaming together doesn't just mean talking about long-term goals, like buying a house or starting a family, although those are important too. It's about imagining a future that both of you are invested in, visualizing how you will grow and support each other along the way. When two people share dreams, they create a common purpose that unites them and gives them direction. It's like building a bridge that connects you forward, making you walk together toward something bigger than each of you alone.

Often, couples forget the importance of sitting down to dream together. Daily routine, responsibilities, and stress can cause them to put aside meaningful conversations about the future. But talking about dreams is not only exciting, it also strengthens the connection. When you sit down with your partner and share what you want to achieve, you are telling them that you trust them and want them to be a part of your life. Plus, by listening to your partner's dreams, you show them that you care and that you are willing to support them in what they want most.

A good place to start when talking about shared dreams is to remember what you once imagined together. Perhaps, at the beginning of your relationship, you had exciting plans that you put aside over time. Talk about those ideas. Do you still want to pursue them? If so, what can you do to get back to them? If not, what new dreams have emerged? These kinds of conversations not only renew the spark, but they also remind you of what unites you.

It's important that you both have the freedom to express what you really want, even if your dreams seem different at first. For example, one of you might dream of traveling the world while the other wants to settle down in a stable place. This doesn't mean that your dreams are incompatible. With communication and creativity, you can find ways to combine both visions. Maybe you can travel for a while before settling down or find a balance that satisfies both of you. The crucial thing is to be open to listening and looking for solutions together.

It's also helpful to set concrete goals from those dreams. Talking about wanting to be happy or successful is fine, but what does that look like in practice? If you want to run a business together, talk about what kind of business you're passionate about, what steps you need to take, and how you can support each other in the process. If you dream of a quiet retirement in the future, what do you need to do now to save or plan for it? Putting details to your dreams makes them more real and attainable.

Not all dreams have to be grand or ambitious. Small shared dreams are just as valuable. Maybe you dream of learning something together, like cooking exotic dishes, playing a sport, or even adopting a pet. These small goals create special moments that strengthen your daily bond. Plus, by achieving these simpler dreams, you feel motivated to pursue bigger goals.

Sharing dreams also means supporting individual dreams. A relationship doesn't mean giving up what each of you wants for yourself, but rather finding ways to grow together while pursuing your personal interests. If your partner dreams of developing a career or learning something new, support them on that path. Help them find the opportunities they need, celebrate their achievements, and be their biggest cheerleader. By doing so, you're showing that their dreams are important to you because they are important to them.

Like any aspect of a relationship, shared dreams require constant work. What you dreamed of five years ago might not be the same thing you want now. Priorities change, and that's okay. The important thing is to stay in tune and adjust your goals as you evolve as individuals and as a couple. Take time to review your dreams regularly. Talk about what's changed, what's still relevant, and what new desires have emerged.

Also, don't be afraid to dream big. Often, we limit ourselves by thinking that certain dreams are impossible or impractical. But dreaming together isn't just about what you can accomplish — it's about what makes you feel excited and alive. Even if you don't manage to accomplish every dream, the simple act of imagining and planning together creates a deep emotional connection. It makes you feel like a team taking on the world together.

Finally, remember that shared dreams aren't just about the future. They're also about how you enjoy the present as you work toward those goals. Celebrate every step along the way, no matter how small. If you're saving for a trip, celebrate when you hit a milestone in your budget. If you're learning something new together, enjoy the laughter and mistakes that come along the way. Those moments are what turn dreams into valuable memories.

Dreaming together is an act of love and commitment. It's a way to tell your partner that you not only love them today, but that you want to be by their side in the future as well. By sharing dreams, you're creating a path together, filled with goals, accomplishments, and special moments. It's a way to make sure that no matter what happens, you'll always have something to work toward and something to be excited about, together.

Letting Go To Move Forward

Letting go in order to move forward is one of the most challenging, but also most transformative, lessons in a relationship. We often carry emotional baggage that accumulates over time: resentments, disappointments, words spoken in moments of anger, or wounds we haven't been able to heal. This invisible weight not only drains our energy, but also creates barriers between us and our partner. Letting go doesn't mean ignoring what happened or minimizing feelings. It's a conscious act of releasing the past to build a lighter, happier future.

First, it's important to identify what you're carrying. Maybe there's a memory that keeps coming up in arguments. Maybe you feel like you haven't been able to get over a betrayal, or there's something your partner did long ago that still hurts you. Reflect on these feelings and be honest with yourself. What exactly is it that's bothering you? Is it something that happened once, or is it a pattern that hasn't been resolved? Before you can let go, you need to recognize what it is that you're holding on to.

Talking about these issues with your partner is a crucial step. Keeping resentment in silence only makes it grow. But at the same time, it's important to approach these conversations from a place of calm, not confrontation. Use a quiet moment to express how you feel. For example, instead of accusing, you can say something like, "I've realized that there's something that's still bothering me, and I want to talk about it with you because I want us to be better." This openness creates a safe space for communication and prevents the conversation from turning into a fight.

The process of letting go also requires empathy. Often, the pain we feel is related to actions or words from our partner that may not have been intentional. Try to put yourself in their shoes. Ask yourself if what they did was a human error or if there was a lack of mutual understanding. This doesn't mean justifying harmful behavior, but it does help you see the situation from a broader perspective. Empathy can soften intense emotions and open the door to forgiveness.

Forgiveness, of course, is at the core of letting go. Forgiveness isn't saying that what happened is okay, nor is it forgetting. It's a conscious decision to not let the pain control your life or your relationship. It's letting go of the need to punish your partner or keep reminding them of what they did. Forgiveness is a gift you give to yourself as much as it is to the other person. It's freeing yourself from the weight that ties you to the past so you can move forward.

Letting go also involves learning from experiences. Every challenge in a relationship has something to teach us, whether it's about our own needs, how to communicate better, or what we value in our partner. Reflect on what you can take away from those experiences, but without getting stuck in them. Think about how you can apply those lessons to strengthen your relationship in the future.

On the other hand, it's important to accept that not all wounds can be healed right away. Some things need time, and that's okay. Don't put pressure on yourself to let go overnight. What's important is that you're working toward that goal, taking small steps each day. Maybe one day you'll be able to talk about it without feeling so much pain, or maybe one day you'll realize that you don't think about it as often anymore. Celebrate those small steps forward.

Sometimes, we need to let go of our own expectations, too. In a relationship, it's common to create an image of what our partner should be like or how they should behave. But no one is perfect, and we all make mistakes. If you hold on to a rigid idea of how things should be, you're closing yourself off from the possibility of accepting and loving your partner as they are. Letting go of these expectations doesn't mean settling, but rather being more flexible and realistic in your expectations.

Finally, remember that letting go is not something you do just for your partner. You do it for yourself. Accumulated resentment and pain not only affect the relationship, but also you as an individual. Letting go is freeing yourself from that emotional burden that prevents you from being fully happy. It is allowing yourself to enjoy the present without the past clouding your vision. It is choosing peace instead of conflict.

Letting go in order to move forward is an act of love, both toward your partner and yourself. It's a way of saying that the past will not define the future, that you're willing to do the work necessary to build something stronger and more beautiful. It takes courage and commitment, but the results are worth every effort. When you choose to let go of what's holding you back, you open up space for the love, understanding, and connection you so desire to flourish. And in that process, you discover that, in the end, letting go is a way to win.

Love in Constant Construction

Love in a relationship is not something you build once and it stays perfect forever. It is a constantly evolving project, like a house that always needs care, repairs, and sometimes a complete renovation. Thinking that a relationship can sustain itself, without effort, is a common mistake. Love needs daily dedication, attention to detail, and a mutual commitment to keep it alive and strong. When we accept this reality, we can approach our relationship with a more positive and constructive mindset.

The first step to continually building love is to remember that no relationship is perfect. We all have bad days, make mistakes, and face challenges. These moments are not the end of love, but rather opportunities to strengthen it. Instead of seeing difficulties as insurmountable obstacles, we should look at them as bricks that, when placed with patience and care, can form the foundation of a stronger relationship. For example, an unresolved argument can become a wall between you, but if addressed with communication and empathy, it can transform into a bridge that connects you more deeply.

Daily effort is essential. We often think that big declarations of love, like a special trip or an expensive gift, are what really matters. While those moments are beautiful, love is also built in the small, everyday gestures. Making breakfast, listening attentively after a long day, or simply saying "I love you" for no apparent reason are ways to consistently show love. These gestures, even though they may seem simple, are what keep the spark alive and strengthen the bond.

Building love also requires quality time together. In a world full of distractions, such as work, social media, and other responsibilities, it's easy to lose sight of how important it is to spend time with your partner. This time doesn't have to be elaborate. It can be something as simple as sitting down to watch a movie together, going for a walk, or sharing an uninterrupted meal. The important thing is to be present — not just physically, but emotionally and mentally.

Another crucial aspect is adaptability. Relationships change over time, just like people. The couple you were at the beginning may not be the same after a few years, and that's okay. The important thing is to grow together, not grow apart. This means being willing to adapt to your partner's changes and accepting that love can evolve, too. Maybe you used to enjoy going out to parties, and now you prefer quiet nights at home. Maybe priorities have changed over time. The important thing is to embrace these changes rather than resist them.

Patience is another key pillar. There will be days when things don't go as planned, when you feel frustrated, or when the connection seems weak. In those times, it's important to remember that love doesn't always feel perfect, but that doesn't mean it's not there. Patience helps you get through the tough times without giving up. It's knowing that even though there are storms, the sky will eventually clear if you're both willing to work together.

Gratitude also plays a huge role in the ongoing building of love. It's easy to take your partner for granted after a while. However, taking a moment to appreciate what they do for you, what they bring to your life, and what they mean to you can completely change your perspective. Saying "thank you" sincerely, acknowledging their efforts, and showing appreciation are all ways to keep your relationship fresh and loving.

Building love also involves learning and growing together. This can be as simple as reading a book you both are interested in or taking a class together, to tackling important challenges as a couple. Each shared experience becomes another brick in the structure of your relationship. The more experiences you share, the stronger the love you build.

Ultimately, building love in a relationship is an act of daily choice. Every day you have the opportunity to choose your partner anew, to show them that they are important to you, to work on strengthening your connection. It's easy to get carried away by routine and forget about this aspect, but when you take the time to consciously choose your partner every day, love becomes something alive and dynamic.

Loving in constant construction is not easy. It requires effort, dedication, and a genuine commitment. But the result is worth it. A relationship built with care and attention not only stands the test of time, but also flourishes, providing joy, support, and a deep sense of connection. In the end, love is not a destination, but a journey, and every step you take together is an opportunity to build something truly beautiful.